THIS CHANGES THINGS

Claire Askew was born in 1986 and grew up in the rural Scottish borders. She has lived in Edinburgh since 2004, and holds a PhD in Creative Writing & Contemporary Women's Poetry from the University of Edinburgh. In 2013 she won the International Salt Prize for Poetry, and in 2014 was runner-up for the inaugural Edwin Morgan Poetry Award for Scottish poets under 30. Her first book-length collection, *This changes things*, was published by Bloodaxe in 2016. She runs the One Night Stanzas blog, and collects old typewriters (she currently has around 30).

CLAIRE ASKEW

THIS CHANGES THINGS

BLOODAXE BOOKS

ISBN: 978 1 78037 276 1

First published 2016 by
Bloodaxe Books Ltd,
Eastburn,
South Park,
Hexham,
Northumberland NE46 1BS.

www.bloodaxebooks.com
For further information about Bloodaxe titles
please visit our website or write to
the above address for a catalogue.

Supported using public funding by
ARTS COUNCIL
ENGLAND

Cover design: Neil Astley & Pamela Robertson-Pearce.

Printed in Great Britain by Bell & Bain Limited, Glasgow, Scotland, on
acid-free paper sourced from mills with FSC chain of custody certification.

In memory of Robert Alan Robinson,
1927–2015

CONTENTS

Dukkha

Shelter is the only really necessary thing.
Every creature has its burrow,
bolt hole, cave, its fist of twigs.
Just make it safe, a place
above the flood plain: shake
its sticks and slates to test
it can withstand a storm. That's all.

That, and water somewhere near,
the good, clear kind that scrubs itself
clean through the stones and flows
all year without a freeze. Some fish.
Some trees. A nesting bird for eggs.
Some plants, a patch of dirt,
some basic tools. A shovel and a pan.

But then, your square of soil might spoil
its seeds. You'll need blades, some kind
of beast to slug them through the mud
in rows. You'll need to feed it
from your grain: this changes things.
You'll need some cloth.
You'll need to cut a bigger plot.

Now there must be hands to help:
more hands, more mouths.
The shelter shrinks, the feed bags thin,
you need a needle, thread, a pot,
a kiln, a cart. There must be
markets, good roads leading in.
You'll need a lamp. You'll need a gun.

You'll need a coin. You'll need
a tin to keep your coins inside.
You'll need a man to guard the tin.
Give him your gun and get another.
Make your shelter taller, stronger.
Now you have an acre, need
an engine, need an engine shed.

Now fuel: a sticky, black-eyed well.
A slaughterhouse, a pit for rotting things,
incinerator, chimneys made of brick,
cement. Good rivets, chicken wire –
no, barbed. A guard. Electric current,
cashflow. Long flat cabins
for your hired hands. A bank.

The shelter must be strong,
the water pure. The soil must nurture
tall, true wheat, the hands work
till the yield is in. The lamp must strike,
the gun must kill its target cleanly.
This is all you want.
This is all that anyone wants.

I

I'm sorry I'm still in love with my grandmother

I'm sorry I'm still in love with my grandmother.
Creature in curlers, who never scoured
the pans to your liking; who collected
the milk off the step in her slip
and stockings at seventy; who'd take off
her shoe – stiletto or slipper – to skelp
an unruly dog. I'm sorry I'm still in love.

With my grandmother, everything was done
to extremes. The Christmas puddings, flooded
with brandy; the flames she kindled,
a kimono'd Moloch. Cigarettes, their spent ends
strewn from sink to sofa; the stove with its soup,
and the grate with a fresh glow at 5 a.m. –
the house always hot as hell. I'm sorry,

I'm still in love with my grandmother,
having been plied with shortbread
and sausage-meat sandwiches, too small
to know better. I was seduced
by the photo-albums, the jewellery box –
by the sweet-shop, the swing-park,
the shopping centre. She had so many strategies.

I'm sorry I'm still. In love with my grandmother
is a strange place to be, with a slew of soil
between us now, and only her smoke
from that final, brilliant fire
in the sky overhead.

Big heat

If I move now, the sun
naked between the trees
will melt me as I lie.

ADRIENNE RICH

Because I am the one who speaks English,
they call me outside.
In the street, in an elbow of weak light
thrown by our porch, two tourists
mumble like fat, white grubs.
The boy comes up the steps to me,
hand round a bad map someone drew.
His face is hot, red, wet as a tongue.

The girl is crying. They are looking
for a house that, when they find it,
will be shuttered, lime-scale white
and dry. I want to say
that crying is a stupid luxury
the island women can't afford:
I trained my babies early
not to dehydrate themselves this way.

I know it will be morning now
before this girl, her massive backpack
full of useless things, can find
the market, buy a quart
and pull that water back
inside herself again. But I'm quiet,
pour a glassful for her from our fridge.
She sputters *thank you* in our language.

Things that thrive here: mules
and stones, crickets loud as fire alarms,
the harder vines. Old women
whose hands and feet are tough,
whose men worked boats or built homes
all day in the big heat,
and died young. The boring sun.
Slow flies the size of grapes.

My father finds the torch and guides them
down the street's steep shoulder,
holding the light down round their feet,
until they are out of sight.
All night, under the chattering fans,
I think about the girl's chapped throat,
the boy she lies beside,
their mouths. None of us sleeps.

Anne Askew's ashes

All day, the stove has sulked and spat, sucking hard
on knucklebones of coal. I shed my coat and kneel to sift the ash
between the grate's iron teeth – restack the fire-bricks,
sweep and scrape – to reinflate this blackened lung.

When I am done, my wrists are rigor-mortis grey
and ringed with soot like rope-burns, shackles,
marks of prayer. In the backyard's bitter air,
the ash-pan stutters, spills itself a little in the wind.

I make it to the bin and tilt the pan,
release a ghoul of smut and dust that dirls and hangs there
after I am gone. A blazing witch, now silent as the earth –
you are the ghost in every fire I birth.

Hometown

Last week a horse drowned in the Junction Pool.
Already it's an urban myth you don't believe:
the river still and thick and stinking
underneath its parasol of evening flies.
You're in the square. You're counting out
a pocket of shrapnel by the cheap white light
of Tweeddale Tackle's shuttered front.
Round here, the shops are lit like beacons
every single night, and locals lie
that no one needs to lock their doors.

The next bus won't be here for hours.
Outside the Cross Keys, limos start to roll up
for the sixth-year prom, drawing listless drunks
out to the steps of all the nearby bars.
You hang moth-like outside the chip shop,
boredom scuffing your school uniform.

Down on the Cobby path the summer nettles
swallow trolleys whole. The sound of tape-recorded bells
hangs in the graveyard yew trees' grown-out perms.
Boy racers burn their good tyres into useless slicks
broadsiding through the lorry park.
You cheggle off your fringe with safety scissors
in the public loo, wait in the darkening bus stop for anything.
You get home as the street lights start their on-off
orange flirting with the trees. Your sister says
if you don't leave this town when you grow up then I will break your knees.

High school

Better than the fractions like weird pictograms,
better than *Othello*'s major themes, the queens
and kings of Scotland down the years,
titration, verbs in conjugation tables
you can still recite – the sound let out
before the thought's complete – *Je suis.*
Tu es. Il est. Elle est. What you learned best
was the fact of your disgustingness.

How vile you were. Your every flaw:
the monstrous, speckled thighs that brimmed
from gym shorts, ringed with red elastic welts
and howled down in the changing rooms.
The shoes: too flat, too high
you slattern, too gum-soled and scuffed,
or not enough. The hairstyle that your Mum
still cut; your Mum; the blush of rage

or shame that spread routinely up
your neck. Your ugly neck. Your neck,
never adorned with friendship beads or later,
hickies. Your score of same; of love notes
passed to you in class, slow dances, gropings,
fucks – all zero – kept with everyone's for broadcast
in the midst of something good, the way
a dying rock star breaks the evening news.

It's women who learn first the throw that hurts,
the way to really wound your fellow girl,
the soft parts where it doesn't show
and cannot heal. How did these blue-eyed whippets
learn so much of power and spite in years
you'd spent just grooming dolls and waiting,
fanning gravel out behind your bike's
bald, beaded, tinkling wheels?

The worst thing: they believed it all,
the tiny hierarchies built and smashed
at rum-and-cola parties you were never party to.
They thought that life would always hold
the door for them, or for their looks, their smart
high-kicks – did it matter which? – and you'd always be
some chubby joke. You believed it too.
The softest part of you believes it now.

The lucky little girls

The valley was filled with things that should have frightened us:
leeches in the Bowmont, ticks clinging in the grass.
Combines dipping like warships through the ripe wheat,
green clouds over Kelsocleuch, their guy-ropes of lightning.

Nothing was forbidden but the ruined
shepherd's cottage on the Law,
the gubbed skull of its walls
a smudge in the high trees.

It felt like miles from the village, dragging our preteen boredom
past the roofless barn with crossbeams like a warning,
stink of rotted hay inside. Autumn, and that track ran like a beck.
Summer whacked our legs with goosegrass stalks.

We called it the haunted house, as though its family
of imagined ghosts were why we weren't allowed.
Every winter ripped more slates out of the roof
to stand up in the dirt like little graves.

Did we ever go inside? My memories
are of waiting at the nettled fringe beyond the fence,
and looking in at peeling tiles, a fireplace,
door jambs hanging sagged and wrong.

We knew nothing. Too young to read the paper, doing homework
through the TV news. The worst things that happened
to children we knew involved bruises, or tattoos made with biros
and a tailor's pin. We laughed in the face of a fucked world run by men.

But we felt it there, a click or so away from home,
each egging all the others on to go inside.
Fear: real and glassy as a lake,
though reassuring sunlight zazzed on everything.

We were the lucky little girls, I know that now. We'd find
a reason to turn back – the sound of thunder up at Kelsocleuch –
a thing we could outrun. Lucky to grow, and learn to be afraid,
before that house became the famous site of something bad.

Catalogue of my grandmother's sayings

A bloody good hiding
Another egg chipped
Bent as a nine-bob note
Blood and sand
Blood and stomach pills
Broad as it's long
Brought up in the bottle and seen nowt but the cork
Could ride bare-arsed to London on them scissors
Could've written *slut* in the dust in that house
Dogs in the same street bark alike
Good clip under the lug's what he needs
Like a blue-arsed fly
Ninepence to the shilling
Not as green as he's cabbage-looking
Queer as Dick's hatband
Six of one and half a dozen of the other
Twined as a bag of weasels
Well go to the foot of our stairs
Well our Helen Judith Sarah Christine Claire
What a right bag of washing
You want nowt with that I tell you
You want nowt with that

To Wakefield

(after Jenny Lindsay)

Wakefield, you dirty bitch.
You patron saint of brickyards and rickets,
leaky filling in the mouth of the North.
There is no better word for you than *slag*.
Sat out on the dead and yellow lawn
of industry, braless and drunk,
you're hitching up your negligee
to flash the trains.

Wakefield, the ultimate lousy lay –
mutton-dressed catastrophe, shoving your hands
down the jeans of strangers in doorways
on the Westgate run, and hiccupping kisses at Leeds.
Wakefield, you brash and brass-necked slattern
whose tongue is the Saturday turn
at the Working Men's Club
and whose stockings have run at the seams.

Shaky Wakey – your phone number inked
in the single stall of the gents
at the Cock and Dolphin
alongside the words *for a good time call…*
Wakefield. You fag-end of cities;
you district of many a dirty black mouth,
all stoppered now and blowsy with hate.
Wakefield, you flag-decked capital of chavs.

I told you I loved you.
You punched my lights out and fucked my Dad.

Visiting Nannie Gray

We go on Sundays to make her tea.
I've known her years, but every week
we're introduced. She thrums my name's soft hiss
in her teeth, tells you she's sure
you and I are for keeps.

We bite our lips as she slams round the house,
chitters for a long-dead cat, and
worried he's missing, puts out fish.
She never sits –

fluttering like a moth at the nets,
she asks you where we've tied the horse
and trap, while the red Ford Escort smarts in the drive
like a wound.

And would I like to see her frocks?
And every week I say I would.

She spreads them on the bed like relics,
recites the names of seamstresses, department stores.
There's always one whose floral print
she bunches in her fist – flimsy anchor to the past –
says without flinching, bury me in this.

And that's the moment every week,
the heart-stuck lurch as she realises what she is,
for just a breath. Then like a child, afraid and angry,
she reaches for me, whispers *I'm sorry.*
I'm sorry.

Frank

is quiet at his window,
cut by his Double Two shirt,
the slices of the old blind,
sunlight jutting in.
He's often there, watching the year
assert itself: magpies lining their smart black coats
with light, daffodils setting up camp.

Captain Frank, retired, is 84.
He has no car, no dog
and no TV, but lives
the tiny dramas of the street.
It's Frank who sugars grit along the path
before the snowfall comes.
It's Frank who takes in everybody's bins.

I looked up once from stacking wood
and found him at the front gate
with a gift for me: two ancient, dark red bricks.
A storm is on its way, he said.
Tie everything down.

All day I watch Frank's house – identical
to mine – but no one comes or goes.
All day I wear the same stripe back
and forth across the pale straw rug.

Frank stands and tracks the movement
of the crows, the local dogs, the bin man's truck.
Beyond the street the yards are full of fitted sheets
inflating on their whirligigs.

At night the wind plays sad trombones
under the eaves. I have the same recurring dream:
the houses shed their blotchy pebbledash
and blow away like paper lamps.
All except for mine and Frank's.

Spitfires

Impossible,
to think he was once seventeen –
the man in the solid coffin,
no longer a man, no longer my grandfather, really
just a body –
too young
to serve – amazing, that he was once too young
for something – so he fixed Spitfires,
those beautiful death machines,
all Blitz pitch, all rivets.
Imagine the big wings, the heat fizz off the airfield –
taxiing a patched rig across the hardstanding
to see if she'd go –
the snubbed guns, ritzy pin-ups
on the buttressed nose.
Fighting bulldogs in their clotted greens.
He loved them seventy gentle years,
and now behind a curtain the coffin burns,
and he walks out of the hangar
in the teatime light.
He knocks his hands together once,
twice, three times. Behind him,
empty Spitfires huge as windmills
in a quiet row. He whistles,
and he's seventeen.

Going next

It happens as we're driving back
from another day clearing
my grandfather's house.

It's Christmastime, and from the rise
all the little hamlets of the valley
are lit like pinwheels.

All day we've packed boxes in the cold house,
everything damp, our breath standing in the air
reminding us every two seconds that we are alive.

Now we're driving through the black late afternoon,
the wind swinging in the trees like it wants to hurt them,
the trees swatting back with their long sticks.

And my father says, *now that he's dead*
I'm the eldest, out of nowhere in the hot,
thick air of the car. *I'm going next.*

He says it
like the thought has suddenly come –
keeps his hands on the wheel and doesn't speak again.

And I'm surprised he thinks
I don't know him better,
I don't know

he's been thinking it all these weeks,
as we've stacked books, made tramp tea
in a pan on the single gas ring,

as we've surfed together on the loose boards
of the old man's loft, laughing at the things he kept,
the crap raft of stuff he built for himself.

In his head, my dad has walked
to the end of that familiar street,
but instead of scuffing the chalked brick

of the last house – outpost beyond which
he wasn't allowed – then running back
to his name called ahead of the dark,

he's turned. The road beyond the corner
is new, and the houses are low,
so although it's still far off he can see it,

perhaps it's a tower,
or a spire, or a plume of grey smoke
drifting slow above the rooftops of the town,

but he knows this is where he's going now,
and the road is straight, and there's no one there any more
to call him home.

Thing about death

The worst thing about death must be the first night.

JUAN RAMÓN JIMÉNEZ

The worst thing about death must be the first night:
spluttering awake, so blank in the absence of sweat
or the regular high-kick of a pulse,
the grainy playback of your life refusing to quit
on its endless, pointless loop.
The worst thing about death must be the quiet.

The worst thing about death must be
having to walk around with all
the undertaker's greasepaint still on your face.
The worst thing about death must be
constantly singeing your fingers on matchsticks
trying to light the cigarette you cannot taste,
the nerve endings of all your extremities dead
like everything else, though you never remember.

The worst thing about death must be forgetfulness.
The worst thing about death must be
the time to sit alone with your regrets.
The worst thing about death must be
knowing now that no regrets
is just one of many sugar-coated lies the living tell.
The worst thing about death must be,
eventually, the smell.

The worst thing about death must be
the truly weird things you miss: psoriasis
and heartbreak, buses, seagulls, flip-flops,
anarchists at dinner parties, all the dogs you ever owned.
Your car. The junk collected in a bedside drawer
then thrown away – you wish you'd kept it now.

The worst thing about death must be
the rotting flowers giving way
to unkempt grass and less and less
footfall, mourning, memory, or sense of loss.
The worst thing about death must be
the aggravating lack of clocks.
The worst thing about death must be
the constant dark, its unforgiving yawn.

The worst thing about death must be the first night
you know you did not dream of living.

Poltergeistrix

First, she watches her lover's grief
with tasty horror. When he lies
face down and foghorns out her name,
she places her weightlessness along him,
sinks her fist into his chest
and rummages, touching the shuddering lungs
in turn, the heart chugging down
its jello-shots of blood.

She loves that she is presence
without mass: her pass says
access all areas and she does,
sampling all the things he'd not
be seen dead doing. Within a week,
she learns he likes his porn vanilla,
blonde and young; that when he comes
alone he wears a different face.

But without her, he's thuddingly dull.
After a month she's done
going bump in the night, writing
love notes in his minging human dust.
The pizza cartons piling up,
mugs scumming green and grey
till he runs out and buys a slub
of plastic party cups, the final straw.

It's been weeks now, but he's still
so lousy with the snot and tears
and stench of death, it's gross.
I want to see other ghosts, she says,
it's over – but he doesn't even flinch.
She spends a final night, fingering
things she'll miss: gilt picture frames,
a silver brooch, the cat. Not him.

By dawn, she's gone. Now being dead
is fun: she melts through buildings floor by floor
the way a good knife butchers wedding cake.
But the more she poltergeists around, the less
she's human: soon she's gawping through
their windows like this city is a massive,
boring zoo. They're all the same.
Dysfunctional, but ultimately dull as rust.

She gives up: finds a crypt whose lock is good.
There'll be no piss-stink, no kids crawling in
to smoke and fuck, just leaf mould
and the local dead. She's heard you get
a dying wish, and saved hers up,
but now she speaks it to the hunkered stumps,
the graveyard and its scary sky. *Make sure
he never finds me. Better: never let him die.*

The minister sees the monster

It was a wet summer:
the village a damp fort surrounded
by field water. Four o'clock I was up –
the grey light punched and wrung –
like it had called me, like it needed to be seen.

I'm not a walker, but with stick and boots
and picked-thin overcoat I went.
Under the backfiring streetlights,
over the green with the dawn sky
turning like milk.

By the chapel the river was loud.
By the dyke the path was addled
with the glyphs of many hooves.
In the hedge birds quipped and flinched.
My boots turned black in the damp.

I cut round a ditch loosed
and pooled by rain.
On Cemetery Road
there's a gate I climbed,
slipping, giggling adrenaline.

Though it made no sound I turned there,
the old, hot wire of fear pulled taut,
and saw it through the blown thorns
for a moment. Long enough to know
that it was grey, and larger than a dog.

I inferred teeth. I cut home through the graves
for cover, wet white fog rising
round the houses like a useless keep.
I haven't told the village. I believe
whatever comes is what's deserved.

Picker

Here she is: midnight, tightroping
along the skip's thin side
in plimsolls, dead man's overcoat.

Some weird beast on birdlegs
with a torch's orb
strapped anglerfish style,

she's sifting the seafloor
of backyards for builders' scrap,
lagging, hotwater tanks.

Her van's on the next street:
keys in, ready for the peel out
and the getaway —

old model with the lorry clutch,
her left knee up
somewhere round her ear

to make the racing changes
through this estate's
crazygolf of roundabouts.

She's found a greenhouse,
frame stuck skyward
like a scuppered ship,

ten good panes she stacks
against the skip's bowed side
like vinyl LPs.

This woman loves a length of pipe
like other women love shoes.
She comes gloved,

hands pumiced by breezeblocks:
boltcutter and needlenose pliers
her answer to everything.

You're imagining her life:
nocturnal reader of small ads,
whistler at foxes,

loner, flat full of old shit
nobody wants. Cut glass ashtrays
the size of cheeseplates,

racks of plasterboard, a shifting smell.
You're miles off. She's already
in the driver's seat,

the outline of the van's scrubbed
Royal Mail decals showing up
under lamppost fake-tan light.

She turns the keys gone cold
in the ignition and the dash clock
tells her it's tomorrow.

She trusts it, kicking up
through the gears. She's a thief.
A thief trusts everyone.

Onion

(after Carol Ann Duffy's 'Valentine')

This year, it's personal: I'm giving you
the dirtiest of Valentines. This:
a bulge of hard and sapling flesh
unsheathing from its grotesque
loop of hair. It crackles
as you tear away its homespun shirt
and start a sweet undressing –
dance of a thousand foreskins,
luminous and slick. Unzip it
with your grinning blade and see it
spill apart to offer you
the tarnished earring-hoops of strippers,
pregnant girls in chip shop queues.
I'm carving up this clutch
of pawnshop jewels so you can glitter
filthily. I'm slipping you this sticky fist
to see you spent
and breathless with delicious tears.
I'll cross your palm with slivers
of my gift so you can wear
the guilty stink of its secretions
on your fingertips long afterwards,
perhaps for days. I've cut its heart out,
held it in my teeth. I'll leave you
with its tongue still in your mouth.

Privilege 101

It's knowing how much cash you can put on a horse
without caring if you win. It's winning,
then giving a little to the man in the doorway
round the side of the track, then telling everyone
at dinner you gave it to him. It's the noise they make
when you finish the tale. It's cufflinks and silverware,
a waitress who takes your coat;
it's whether or not you acknowledge her, that choice.
It's dinner, not really worked for or worried about; the tip
you chuck in the tray on your way out.

It's sitting in the window of a coffee shop, the sun
painting bars across the wooden floor, the plain steel
flip-top teapots shining, writing down ideas that are all yours.
It's walking out of there, blue notebook under your arm,
into the lean summer afternoon without fear,
and choosing which of those ideas you share with whom.
It's the way the off-licence cashier addresses you,
his hazel eyes meeting your own, the fact he doesn't
follow as you head through to the better whisky
lined up in its amber jars.

It's skin you wear each day with all its flaws, adornments;
taut and fine as corset lace. Desirable.
Your place on the massive swatch-chart you call race.
It's limbs, their length and shape, the ground you cover easily,
the measured stretch to catch the hard-stitched ball that's thrown,
your fingers maple-leafing out to fling it back. It's the park
where all of this is done, the quiet, clipped grass,
the landscaped trees the afternoon hangs in
like chimes. It's the streets you climb when you go home,
shutters rolling down as lights blink on above your head in globes.

It's home: four walls you pull around yourself no matter
what the day has done. They're walls you picked yourself
and painted, hung with lamps and scraps and gems,
your things. It's things like this, and simpler: shoes.
A bank account that bears your name. An obelisk
of shelves with books, fist of keys you didn't steal,
a passport and a roll of coins. It's death,
the one that you will someday get: a grave
to visit, watered, free of weeds. It's all of these:
these hair's-breadth tricks of fortune, birth and place.

So random, yet it's rampant in your blood.
It begs to be checked.

Fire comes

Fire comes to the garden like a sordid thought, brought by a hand
    starfishing out
to ditch a Silk Cut filter still alight. It can't believe its luck: a smudge
    of creosote
spilled up a wall, a windless night, the brown grass stiff as hackles,
    ankle deep
and stirred by ticks that fizz and burst like cereal in Fire's mouth.
    It rises,
slides its greasy back against the fencing slats, unfocuses the garden
    in a haar
of smoke. Beyond the helpless trees somewhere a dog rattles awake;
    the air brake
of a distant night bus seethes. Fire slides its tongue into the house's
    ear.

This is where the delicacies are: long flanks of cloth that Fire can
    hoover up.
Stuffed furnishings, their safety labels powerless as lucky charms;
    the carpets thick
and edible as bread. In folded quiet, Fire gums the skirting-boards,
    flirts briefly
with its own reflection in the triple-mirrored gas-fire's front. In the
    hall it pauses,
shorts the fuse box; stops the shrill, pinched pinging of the smoke
    alarm and pulls
the walls down round its shoulders like a cape of dark. Now every
    downstairs room
is Fire's. The windows blow. The faces of the white goods melt like
    cheese.

Upstairs, the woman holds the house's only heartbeat in her clotted
    chest.
The varnished floorboards spit and pop while smoke gritty as candy-
    floss
redraws the room. She's coldly calm: though Fire is taking bites
    out of the white,
tiered staircase like it's cake, she can already hear the engines'
    gorgeous, strobing cry
four streets away. All she can think of, crouching down for air the
    way she learned
in school, is all those times she filled out mental lists of things
    she'd save from Fire.
The photographs, the diaries, the cat she thought she'd buy but
    never found or named.

And then the street's a discothèque of blue and red, the neighbours
    on their front steps
in their dressing gowns, the kids agape behind the nets.
And she wants none of it.
And Fire takes it all.

II

The axe of the house

1 *Hacksaw and burn*

The woman who died in this house
went deaf towards the end. Your new neighbour
Mary, clipped in a pinny and pink gloves
like a dinner lady, tells you this
over the fence. The woman's name was June,
you learn. Her smell is on everything:
lavender, talc, menthol and something medical
behind it all. You strip her sixties paper,
carve the carpets up like pie with Stanley knives
then rip them out, tacks flying. She's still
here, her bobby pins wedged in the skirting.
You're learning to do it all gingerly,
feeling her eyes on your neck as you sledgehammer,
hacksaw and burn. You start saying sorry
aloud, splitting floorboards, hauling down
ancient steel blinds that unravel,
clatter like train-wires. But you know
she can't hear you.
She can't hear a goddamn thing.

II *In the dream*

the room is finished.
The dust sheets, pails
of plaster like grey dough,

the toolbox with its bradawl,
spanner, rasp, the lethal
ladder, everything is gone.

You put one palm on a wall
that is cool and smooth.
The room is custard yellow

filled with sun and smells
like fresh banana bread.
Inside, there's only a folding stool

and June, folded down onto it.
Her hair's been done.
She has on white, seamed gloves,

a string of beads like tiny,
iridescent eyes. She says
nothing, though you wait a long time.

Outside, a swift screams low
across the window. Mary's hoover
bothers the adjoining wall

like a big fly. You forget
where you are. Whose house is this?
Who was it invited you in?

III *Deafening*

The open sash throws a kite of late sun
on the boards. Outside,
the fruitless raspberry frisks the wall,
a mother calls a child's name once
across the yards. The next street's
big trees count the fivers of their leaves
in the hot wind. A blackbird in the garden
sings his namesake's Beatles song.

The fridge clicking on, or the clatter
of clapboard shifting in the skip
is enough to scare you half to death.
To think, you lived just weeks ago above the bar:
the late-night chip shop's neon
in your kitchen until 3 a.m. when half the town
came yelling out like gulls into the night-
bus layover chug of your street.

Here, the quiet lies thick and neat
as turf. A siren's painful violin comes drifting
over pampas grass and garage roofs
from miles away. Decades of sleeping through
last call and drunksong, cabs slammed shut
like books, and now you're woken
by the vocal solo of an owl you're certain
can't be real, but is; by foxclaws on the path.

You'll live. You think you'll even come
to love it, though you joke it's deafening.

IV *Mary tells you about the break-in*

They got in with one kick – if you look,
you can still see the boot-mark,
see where the bolt broke – oldest
trick in the book. She liked the house
dark, the rollers down over the nets,
so no one suspected. They left
through the front door like something
official. I heard one of them whistling,
and came from the kitchen to look,
you know we all curtain-twitch
round here, you'll do it too. It was noon,
and the wireless was on and the washer
no doubt swishing away, *you* know.
I thought they were builders,
or gas men – they dressed just the same.
I gave a description of course but
they could have been anyone,
they didn't look like that type.
They took a bit, a bagful, all valuable:
jewellery, stuff they could carry.
Her pin money, a really bonny
silver dish I liked. It wrecked her,
getting back from the day centre
and finding that.
If only I'd known. But I didn't
hear a thing, I swear. Only the whistle,
and the bag, the way it jingled.

v *Housewarming*

You didn't do any of it.
Forgot to bury silver at the threshold.
Forgot a new broom for a new home.
Forgot the salt for long life.
Forgot to bang the pots and shine a light
to frighten old ghosts.

You couldn't bring coals
from the given-up hearth,
though you picture yourself,
absurd at the roadside,
bearing their chack–chack
and spark back in a bucket:

your own crap jack o' lantern.
Your new key hot
from the devil's pocket.

VI *The axe*

You've bought an axe.
It's buried erect and shining,
L of light, in the heart
of the shed. The wind
ekes through the timbers.
You think the shed knows
the reason for the axe.

The blackbird sits on the ridge
of the hip roof. The leaves
of the big trees curl
like brown hands
in your wasted borders.
The skip is taken on a truck.
Autumn rattles the empty canes.

You wonder how many years
you will lie in the dark
like the axe of this house,
its walls turning their backs.
The owl will drop out
of the night, the fox will starve
and open like a bloom.

The white stamens of their bones
on the track. The blackbird long
gone. How many years until
you no longer hear his song?

Rescue industry

Firefighters and tram drivers have undergone specialist training
– to teach them how to remove a dead body from beneath a
tram. The grisly scenario in the event of someone being run
over by a tram is one of 12 "worst case scenarios" that drivers
and those involved with the project have undertaken.

Edinburgh Evening News, April 2014

Late spring. Cherries raffle their pompoms
of blossom along the touchline of the park.

In the peeling coffee shop pashmina'd students cram
for Microeconomics. One says *no, the product's ten* –

her friend lets out an *oh* of terror,
sound like a mower engine shutting down.

Some guy with eyebrows like awkward questions
won't quit staring at me in the queue.

I'll put him in a poem where he loses seven fingers
and an eye, without explaining how.

Everything's diverted: traffic stacked, the Hannibal
sputter of carburetors pushing up the barrel price.

I tune back in as eyebrows guy says *I've never
been given a bouquet in my life*,

and the waitress smiles.
I ought to give up hating men.

Outside, a team of them unpick a mannequin
from the underbelly of a tram,

take turns to kneel and force their breath
into her empty pink plastic bag head.

Royal Mile, the day after the vote

In the big haar we walk to work,
folding the things we are sure of
over and over, smaller and smaller,
until each of us carries their own
creased star of certainty.

This weather makes us neighbours
who don't speak: passing in the dawn fog
without looking, doing nothing
though we watch the burglary through the nets.
If questioned, we'll say *I did what I thought was right.*

Here are the streets we know:
the squat cathedral daubed with rain,
the unlit shopfront windows with their scarves and tartan
brickproof behind corrugated grilles.
Here is the sunk heart, spat on like a new cut.

This is where we live. Everything graffitied,
the statues chalk-marked like condemned trees,
closes nosing off into a darkness
we don't trust. We stop at the crossing.
Yes, say the lampposts and the downpipes. *Yes.*

Seefew steading

Precarious longhouse:
dislodged, shushing the night
with the dead leaves of sixty winters.

Back field lime-pit:
grave of shot dogs, spina bifida lambs,
victims of snap-leg and foot-rot; ghosts.

One-way half-mile phonebox:
clicking its tongue like a gramophone
unspooled, an old shrew.

Cow in the dark:
foghorn, moose-call, harpy, heavy
old banshee.

Then nothing.
And nothing.

And the river.

Orcas Island

When it rains, you can hear the forest drinking.
On the scabbed veranda, tea cooling in a chipped cup
sends its little breaths up like an offering
to this place made of weather.

Nothing seems to matter but the deer
materialising on the trail
like parlour tricks; the black snake
on the stone steps by the spring.

We sit around like old clocks
winding down, happy to watch for hours
the heads of fog knit in the tops,
the tide pull its wet clingfilm off the stones.

When it rains, it's like the rain
comes from the trees. There is no sky:
around the cabin there's only noise,
the canopy's malachite ring.

In one place on the road out
there's a rise, where the cab driver says
you folks want to make any calls?
If I pull over here you get two bars.

He's the first of us to speak in days:
the phone in his hands like a stone
he might throw. *I drank the rain*, I want to say,
but can't. I've turned into a doe.

Highway: Skagit County, WA

grey welt on the cheek of the land
slap of black duct tape over an old wound
the clouds will not quit worrying the hills
the hills are so sick of one another
everything turns poverty and ominous and bored
there are no voices in the pines
the slopes are thick wet rot and silent
stacked up like a dishrack of forgetting
occasional farms peeled back and stopped
lone bad teeth in a mouth sewn up by the highway
still humming the highway's ugly song

Greyhound, Seattle to San Francisco

Weed, California: elevation 3,425ft above sea level

There's a scrape as he rakes a gear
up from the ancient box's gate
and the bus shoves out of Medford,
Oregon, into the usual great big grey
American dawn. 'California, folks,'
he says as steam or mist or the breath
of early fires sighs up between the foothills' paws.
'Let's all go get high in Weed.'

We ride the hem of a peak he cannot name –
it's 5 a.m. and the mountain throws
a shadow halfway back to Washington.
'Who is this clown and just how long's
he been driving a Greyhound anyhow?'
The radio throws a crackle in his voice
and the whole bus knows
this is a joke grown old long since.

How many sad Americas has he seen,
this stranger we have trusted
to push us safely through the sticky webs
of night? How many terrible
desert casinos flinging infernal neon
at the weary hills? Where are all
the taco serving counter girls
whose names he knows by heart?

Are they spread like thunderclouds
the windshield of his own good sense
can see, and tries to steer against?

Who is this clown, alone under the big-top
indigo nightmare Pacific sky?
He never answers the question.
We pull into Weed, California.
We get high.

The western night

Shove your resplendent sunsets – in these parts, the comedown's fast.
I'm a spoilsport, a real wilful shit –
splashdown on the Pacific's treacly tongue to curdle everything.

I've come to unpick the stitching of another day you doubtless wasted,
waistcoat pockets lined with tricksy knives for cellblock shivs
and unpremeditated alleyways.

And every kid from fourteen down knows I've got horrors:
wardrobe zombies, anacondas loosed from pet stores, psychopaths.
Seems I'm the first mate of pushers and rapists (it's my nature),

and yes, it's true – I'm in the bar-room and the car park
and the lonely road with hands in pockets,
quietly witnessing it all.

And if you think I ever leave you're wrong.
All day I'm underneath the floor, a guilty stink,
or in the attic thinking up unnerving sounds

to play back later. I'll wake you sweating
or shouting or wishing you got that dog
or learned to fire your uncle's gun –

but what's a dog or gun when I've got wolves
and bears, the KGB, late night TV,
vampires, nightmares?

I'll always raise the bet until the world is broke
and naturally I'll show the house I have a royal flush of spades.
Don't ask to see what's up my sleeve – besides, you know.

You name it, I already made it
with the vivid pink Meccano of your race's
collective imagination.

Hello, I'm your personal wire-tapper, extreme body modifier,
amateur pyrotech and by the way
I've gone to the effort of deadening the battery in your smoke
        detector.

Seek me out. Inside the perfect void behind a neon billboard
you can find my footprints in the dirt.
Or just look to the shuddering skyline where I hang my coat.

Parisian hostel

I

Not even that. I'm too ashamed
to let the phrase *a two-bit joint*

roll off my ugly British tongue
but that's exactly

it. Chipboard whitewash
linoleum barebulb candlewick.

I've known you two weeks
and realise the French

I had has loosed
like wool (it takes the trip

for me to note that it's
pardon and not *Entschuldigung*).

Two blocks away they're filling
Gare de l'Est up to the roof

with gas and flares.
It's four in the pitchblack

icy suburb night, we're lost
and looking for a bus.

I look at you and terror
detonates inside my chest.

II

In our anaglypta cheap Bukowski poem of a room
I watch you undress for the first time.
The steam of my breath unfocusses the air.
Your boots uncurl their leafmould sweetmeal smell.
I lie in the picked pink bed.
Like it, I've sat unmade all day
and cooled and warped,
lain giddy for this hour:
the frost's stoppered dusk
in foreign trees and the TVs
in adjacent rooms damped down.
The Métro's rackety passes strung out longer now.
The distant inkspill of the Seine.
I want to slow down time
and hold this moment hard inside my fist:
the whisk and clink as you slip the belt from its loops,
your white feet scuffing the pool of peeled-off clothes.
The heat of you vaselines the freezing window with mist.
You are unfamiliar and magnificent.

Witch

Her trick is to look sane,
look clean, sidle over crablike
so you don't clock her sightless,
milky eye. She must be ninety,
but still looks natty in clamdiggers,
keeps her hair chewed short
to shake the lice. Her smile
is like a once-good plate
smashed and stapled up
along the cracks: age
hasn't wrinkled her, it's hardened
on her surface like a glaze.

She's lived in these sun-trap,
dust-wraith streets
for over six decades,
trailing in the wake of handcarts
at La Boqueria, filching for spilt fish
along the docks until she's sore.
She's got radar for your sort,
and no amount of *no hablo
español* will shake her once
she's tailed you to a leafy square
where yellow light lies
everywhere like dirt.

She finds a cent – its numerals
thumbed flush from all the times
she's pulled this trick –
and licks it, sticks it to her open palm.
The heartline is a rope of muck.
Her thumbs like pulled-up roots.

She sleeps most nights by hiding
in the *jardín* when they lock the gates
and lying by the orange trees
inside the fragrant, violet dark.
She says *dinero*, eclipsing the coin
then showing it again.

Dinero. You give in,
spill out a clutch of change
that's bigger than you'd like.
You see she's wearing plastic
gumball rings on every finger
as she counts aloud,
then tilts off, grinning
like a waxing moon.
Her good eye's on the stretch
of linen tablecloths and silverware.
Her other, mother-of-pearl eye
is fixed on you.

Barcelona diptych

Some people live like this

streets filled with skinny trees
flicking their spring pinks

slim chic flats with lofty
terracotta roofs

every building unshuttered awake
from a thin winter

cool stripes of ironwork
on the balcony's hot tiles

every sash thrown back
and the curtains' gauzy breath

filling the room with fluid light
sky tattered with spires

fountains
flamenco of traffic

the starched skirts of umbrellas
hitched for evening drinks

every step swept
every silver table a saucer of dusk

and up this street
the huge hewn church

unfinished
turning its many faces into the dark

II

Some people live like this –
in the racks of stacked-up
beach apartments, among the Irish bars
and stag-do tours, the sad
late-night t-shirt shops, their *I heart
Barcelona* tat, kids with sunburn
and badges buying sombreros –

old men out late on the main drag
selling bird-whistles, knock-off
designer bags and warm four-packs
of beer, pashminas, fridge magnets,
Catalan flags, everything misspelled
and eager in their brown hands –

their mouths open and close,
they have no Spanish, speak no
English, hate you with your
clean face and good shoes –
you give them nothing even though
they glitter like fishes and speak
in the language of birds.

The picture in your mind when you speak of whores

If it contains a backstreet, nasty alleyway
you wouldn't let your daughter near,
a scum of orange light across the roof
of one cheap, solitary car, then tear it up.
If the focus is on fishnet stockings
pulled with holes and dragging high
into a tatty garter belt, then tear it up.
And tear up too the shiny, slimy, spike-heeled
boots last seen on Cher in 1986,
and then those sci-fi perspex platforms
stocked by the tamer fetish shops.
Tear down the smutty clubs set up by pimps
in purple feathered hats, the upstairs rooms
with torn red lampshades, raided nightly by police.
Tear up the dodgy sepia of gentlemen's clubs.
Tear up the Playboy Mansion, trim and gilt
of huge and spotless yachts cruising the Med:
exclusive hundred thousand dollar nights you read
an exposé about. But equally,
tear up the shipping crates on fishy docks,
vans passing borders in the dark,
the track marks and the crack pipe,
dumpsters, abortions, catfights.
Rip up whatever price you heard,
all those statistics howled in weekend magazines,
what your mate's mate did in Faliraki on his stag,
the tales of fallen high school track stars,
former beauty queens. For godssakes
tear up Julia Roberts and Richard Gere –
and Cleopatra, Mata Hari, Eliot Spitzer,
Mary Magdalene – tear them up, too.
Now speak of whores. Stand in these tatters
of trash and tell these women one thing –
anything – they don't already know.

Mothership

I'm sealed like a threat
in the envelope of a well-made
hotel bed, while the nets
pull up each other's skirts
for passing trucks.
Outside, the pulled-up chug
of traffic lights; a late-night bus's
laboured sackcloth wheeze.

A final spangling bar
of some unpractised karaoke belter.
Blokes. The slam of cabs
and small change spattered
onto paving slabs like hail.
I can hear the banks of daffodils
asleep like clicking light-bulbs,
a lick of river fog along the slates.

Beyond: a freight train's gap-toothed lilt
of *boxcars boxcars boxcars* in the cut.
The last of winter striking out
with boots and stick to die
under the knowing stars.
A pink dawn spilt like paint
up at the barn. A gritty wind.
The year's first wasp fizzing awake.

And way off, if I pin my breath
into my throat, there's also
you. I'm so far out of range
it's sick and threadbare,
but I pick you up.

The ping of your pale beacon
says you're still alive
under the spring night's clammy palm.

Beyond the land's dark shoulder,
and the city's thick refrigerator hum.

Bad moon

The moon must be sick of being in poems –
always gripped by fingers of late honeysuckle,
always filtered in the lake through the jetty's slats,
always silvering the flicked tails of the koi.
Always a dinner plate or mirror,
always a fingernail clipping, a grin.

The moon must be sick of being in poems.
Always the bright pin in the picture's corner,
always looking in at the windows of middle-class homes.
Always shoved above a bridge in Paris or Venice,
always an eyeball or symbol,
always a radiant woman, a bowl.

It's also in the splintered windscreen of the crime scene
with its blots of blood. It's hung over the pig farm,
streaking white across the silo's cheek
and slanting through the lorry walls in blades.
It's in every dented can at the landfill pit,
turning the tip to a shoal of dirty fish.

Never the buried skull,
never the gummed plug in the junkie's sink.
Never the white cat under the truck's wheel,
never the beached and stinking jellyfish.
Never the gallstone or the pulled tooth, of course.
Nobody wants to read poems about this.

Stephen in Waitrose

In the supermarket, Stephen is alarmingly changed.
His usual long and sexy stride
is cut to a shuffle, bafflement
breaking over him like waves.
Dreaming in the strip-lit aisles
he skates from Bakery to Salad Bar
and back, then back again –
imagines the basket in his hand
is my heart, a delicate vessel
for him to fill. The pressure of this
is fit to kill him.

Stephen believes that lists are for the weak.
The fingers of his free, left hand
are always at his lips, or else
he's touching fruit or squeezing bread
as if to test their force. In the supermarket
Stephen talks to everything – the grapes,
the cheese – especially herbs,
the dill and thyme a riddle
he must tease out on his tongue.
The avocados cower in fear of him,
for none is left unpinched.

He shoves into the kitchen flushed, eyes wide,
arms stuffed with bags – it seems
he has been gone for hours.
He unpacks, crushes, chops and cooks,
stopping momentarily to tell me things.
Like once: he said if I were food,
I'd be a cauliflower floret.
I've taken time, digested this –
decided Stephen is an artichoke.
His brilliant shell.
His delicate, edible heart.

Hydra

Everywhere you look is light
so exquisite it hurts. Light
off the taffeta sea, the brief white
rips of wake and surf; light
frosting the bleached houses' sides
wedding-cake perfect; light
in the wires, in the cut pot roofs, light
that's one hundred per cent proof. White-
washed island carefully dressed in light,
bridal; hung with thick sheets of light
like honeycombs, like dress shirts lightly
starched and hung to dry. Yachts in the bite
of the port, marshmallow white,
confettiing armfuls of chopped light
out into water clear and keen as ice.
And over the flat-topped hill as night
comes flirting on, the island saves its great light-
show for last. Ancient, many-headed light
that warms the kilns of myth: clay red, bright
pink, streaked ochre fingering the cloth of sky,
the undersides of all the thin white
clouds turned iris, mauve. And then the fine
pale strings of windows flared like Christmas lights
along the port; yachts flicker and go out, and high
across the strait the pinprick warning lights
flick one by one along the radar masts. Tonight,
insomniac in unfamiliar heat, I'll write
under the moth-bothered kitchen light,
this is the life. Mine is the lightest, easiest life.

ACKNOWLEDGEMENTS

Acknowledgements are due to the editors of the following publications and websites where some of these poems first appeared: *Be the First to Like This: New Scottish Poetry* (Vagabond Voices, 2014), *Best Scottish Poems* (Scottish Poetry Library, 2014), *Caledonian Antisyzygy* (Cordite, 2014), *The Dark Horse, The Edinburgh Review, Furies: a poetry anthology of women warriors* (For Books' Sake, 2014), *Gutter, Hallelujah for 50ft Women: poems about women's relationship to their bodies* (Bloodaxe, 2015), *The Island Review, The Istanbul Review, PANK, Scottish Review of Books, Scottish Sunday Mail, Textualities,* and *Where Rockets Burn Through: Contemporary Science Fiction Poems from the UK* (Penned in the Margins, 2013).

An earlier version of this collection was runner-up for the Edwin Morgan Award in 2014. 'Visiting Nannie Grey' and 'I'm Sorry I'm Still in Love with My Grandmother' first appeared in the pamphlet collection *The Mermaid and the Sailors* (Red Squirrel Press, 2011).

'The minister sees the monster' was shortlisted in the 2015 Buzzwords Poetry Competition, 'Dukkha' for the 2014 Dermot Healy Poetry Prize, and 'Frank' for the 2014 Charles Causley Poetry Prize. 'The lucky little girls' and 'Orcas Island' were longlisted in the 2015 Mslexia Women's Poetry Competition. 'Visiting Nannie Grey' won the 2010 Virginia Warbey Poetry Prize and was published in the prizewinners' anthology. 'Fire Comes' won the 2012 International Salt Prize for Poetry, appeared in *The Salt Book of New Writing 2013,* and won an honourable mention in the 2014 Tom Howard Poetry Competition. 'Hometown' was published on the Scottish Book Trust website as part of their 2014 public participation campaign, Scotland's Stories of Home.

I am grateful to all the above for their support and encouragement, as well as to Dr Alan Gillis and the Department of Creative Writing at the University of Edinburgh; Scottish Book Trust; Creative Scotland's Open Project Fund and the Edwin Morgan Poetry Award, without whom this collection would never have happened. Thanks to Neil Astley, Sarah Ream, Nick Askew, Sally Jubb and Dave Coates for their help in putting together the physical book. Extra special thanks to Stephen Welsh: the only person who gets to read the first drafts.